When You Were Born in China

A Memory Book for Children Adopted from China

By Sara Dorow, with photographs by Stephen Wunrow

Acknowledgments:

Special thanks to Brian Boyd, Kay Johnson, Amy Klatzkin and Susan Caughman, all of whom gave much of themselves to make this a better book than it otherwise would have been.

Steve Wunrow especially wishes to thank Peter Chow, David, Holly, Sherry, Gao Wei, Ma Pei and the wonderful families who allowed him to photograph their adoption experiences in China.

Thanks also to Deborah Talen and Stephen Syrjala for their photographs.

Printed in the United States of America
01 00 99 98 97   10 9 8 7 6 5 4 3 2 1

Publisher Cataloging-in-Publication Data

Dorow, Sara
    When You Were Born in China: a memory book
for children adopted from China / Sara Dorow with
photographs by Stephen Wunrow.
            p.   cm.
ISBN 0-9638472-1-X
1. Chinese American children - Juvenile literature.
2. Adopted Children - United States - Juvenile literature.
[1. Adoption. 2. Chinese Americans.]
I. Wunrow, Stephen, ill. II. Title

HV 875.64.D67   1997   362.7

When You Were Born in China
A Memory Book for Children Adopted from China
ISBN 0-9638472-1-X
Text © 1997 by Sara Dorow
Photographs © 1997 by Stephen Wunrow
All Rights Reserved
Yeong & Yeong Book Company
1368 Michelle Drive
St. Paul, Minnesota 55123-1459
Phone (612) 454-1358; Fax (612) 454-3519

To all the children and parents for whom
the China adoption story is still unfolding.

To my parents, who brought Asia to life.
-SD

To Lori Ming Zhu, Kai Mei, Neli Siew, and the other children
I met in China, and especially for my wife Martha, and our children
Madeleine Soon Young, Emma Elizabeth, and Newell Han Yong.
In loving memory of Lori Ming's mother, Diane.
-SW

The story of when you were born in China is very special.

It is special because it is about you. And because it is about many people who cared for you.

Your story began in China, a huge and amazing and ancient country. No one else has a story exactly like yours, but many other children share part of your story. They are the children like you who were born in China and then adopted by families in other parts of the world.

You probably already know some things about your adoption story. Perhaps you have looked through photos of the city where you first met your mom or dad, or of when you arrived home. Your mom or dad has probably told you about traveling to China to adopt you, and of how wonderful it was to hold you for the first time.

What you might
not know is what
happened before
all that.

You might wonder
where you lived,
what those places
were like, and who
took care of you.

4

This book offers some ideas and pictures that might help you understand the answers to those questions.

Of course, *your* story has some details that are only about you, so they won't be in this book.

There are a few things you should know about China, the country of your birth, because they are important pieces of your story. First of all, China is a very old country with a long history. You may have seen pictures of temples and palaces that are many hundreds of years old.

And everybody
recognizes the Great
Wall, which was
built more than two
thousand years ago.

You can be proud
that you were born
in such a magnificent
country.

You should also know that China is not a rich country. Houses and apartments are small and usually don't have hot running water. In the countryside, people often have no indoor plumbing at all. And most people don't have their own car or telephone.

实施生活垃圾袋装化，促进武林
地区环境工生工作上新台阶！

But China is not a poor country, either. There is enough to eat, and almost everyone has a place to live and a bicycle to get around on. Chinese people save their money very carefully to pay for things like a washing machine, a refrigerator, or a television, or for their child to go to school.

China is also a country that is changing a lot. Many people are moving from the country to the city, where workers are busy constructing buildings and roads. And when people in the city make enough money, they replace their bicycle with a motorcycle or a car.

Tastes are changing, too. Young people might have noodles or dumplings for lunch, then treat themselves to a chocolate ice cream bar or a Coke.

In the countryside, however, families spend most of their money on things like food, clothes, and medicine, and usually don't have enough money to buy anything fancy. They work very hard growing vegetables or grain, raising pigs and chickens, or working in a small factory.

Perhaps most important for the story of when you were born is that China has lots and lots of people. Some years before you were born, the government decided that there were too many people in China. If the population continued to grow, there would be many problems.

It was already very difficult to build enough houses and apartments for every family. And what if many people couldn't find a job? Providing enough food for everyone might be especially difficult.

So China's leaders made some rules. They told mothers and fathers in China that they could have only one child, or sometimes two. That way, the population wouldn't grow so fast. Parents who broke this rule faced serious punishment.

13

People like your birthparents knew this was an important rule, but it was a difficult rule as well. You see, Chinese people love children, and family members are very close to one another. Everybody in the family helps each other out, from kids to grandparents. Parents take good care of their children. When children grow up, they are expected to take good care of their parents! So a family with only one or even two children seems small.

The rule about having only one or two children became even more difficult for your birthparents if you are a girl. In fact, you may have noticed that most of the kids adopted from China are girls. The reason for this may be hard to understand, but it is important to your story.

14

Remember that China is a very old country, so some ideas have been around for thousands of years. One of those ideas is that a son should take care of his parents when they get older. You see, parents usually live with their son until they die. Of course parents love their daughters very much. But if they only have daughters, the daughters will get married

and move away to live with their husbands, where they will help take care of their husbands' parents.

Most people in the countryside do not have enough money to take care of themselves when they get old. So if a mother and father are allowed to have only one or two children, they feel they desperately need at least one son—someone to take care of them when they become too old to work.

But what does this have to do with you? Well, when you were born in China, you may have been born to parents who did not have a son. Your birthparents so much wanted to care for you *and* try to give birth to a son. But having another child would break the government's rule about the number of children they could have in their family, and they would be punished. They would have to pay a very big sum of money, more money than they had. Your birthparents couldn't find a way to keep a daughter in their family and still have a son to take care of them later in life.

There may be other reasons your birthparents could not find a way to care for you in their family.

Some children, whether they are boys or girls, are born with a medical problem that needs fixing. If you are one of those special children, it may be that your birthparents could not afford to pay for a doctor to help make you better. But they knew that somewhere there was a family that could, and it was so important that you get proper treatment and care.

It's also possible that your birthmother was not married, and did not have enough money or help from her family to raise a child by herself.

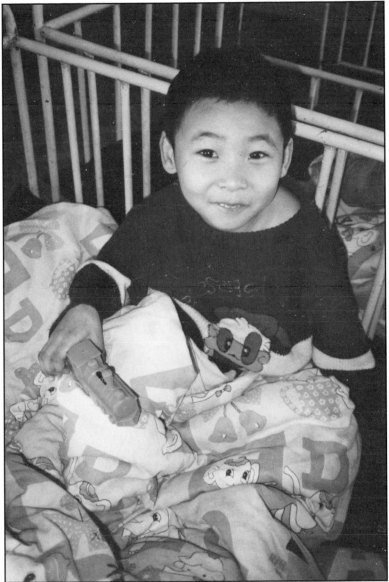

Because you were a precious and beautiful child, your birth family wished with all their hearts that they could keep you with them, care for you, and get to know you. They were heartbroken that they couldn't, and wept at having to say good-bye.

Like many other families in China at the time, your birth family made a very painful decision that another family should take care of you. But China did not have an easy way to help families make an adoption plan. Your parents could get in trouble if they took you straight to an orphanage. So they bundled you up, and maybe put a note in your pocket telling when you were born and explaining that they wanted so much for a family to give you the kind of love and care they couldn't provide.

They then carried you to a public place, like a park, or a busy street corner, or a police station—a place where they knew you would be found by people who could take care of you. And that is exactly what happened!

Someone quickly found you and took you to the police station, because the police would know how to help. There a police officer wrote down information about when and where you were found and then took you to an orphanage, where there were nurses and beds and warm food.

When you arrived at the orphanage, it probably seemed a very busy place. There were many children your age, as well as some younger and some older kids. There were also nurses holding, feeding, and playing with the children. One of these women carried you to the room where you would stay.

Cribs were lined up there, with one or more children in each crib. If it was winter, thick blankets were used to keep you and the other children warm. If it was summer, straw mats were placed in the bottom of each crib to keep you cool. The orphanage nurses may even have cut your hair very short to keep your head cool. (Many buildings in China do not have heat or air conditioning.)

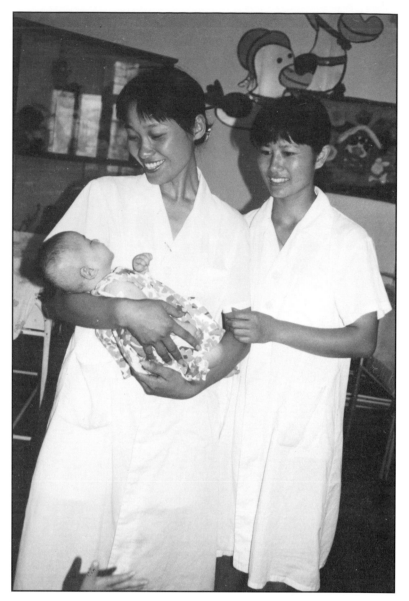

You may have lived at an orphanage for a few months, or maybe even for several years. During that time, the nurses loved and cared for you, and hoped for the day when you would have your own family.

Your room and the people in it became very familiar to you, and you got used to being fed and changed at certain times. When it was time to eat, the nurses mixed milk powder with boiled water, maybe adding some rice cereal or an egg, and filled the bottles. A bottle was then popped into each baby's mouth. Sometimes the nurses used chopsticks to feed the children.

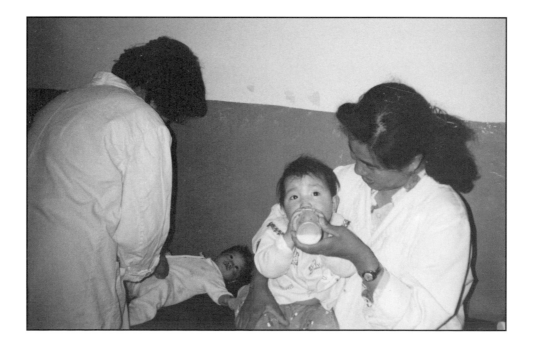

Of course you wore diapers, but not for long. When you were a few months old, you probably started to wear split pants—pants that were open under your bottom. Every so often, a nurse held you over a potty chair. If you were old enough, the nurses would set you right on it.

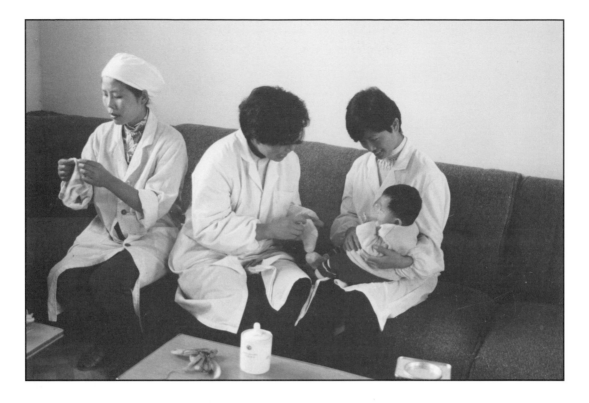

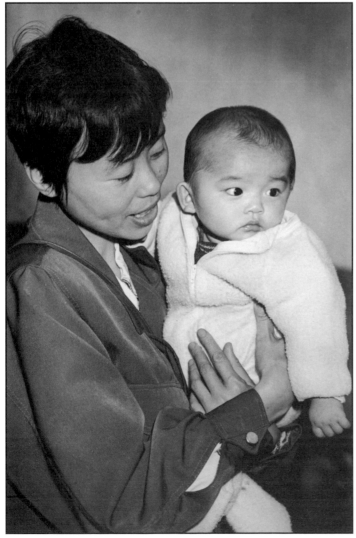

You got a bath now and then, too, when a nurse would dip a cloth in warm water and wipe your hands and face and body. When they had time, the nurses washed your clothes by hand and hung them out to dry.

The nurses were busy looking after so many children. But they held you and played with you as often as they could, and smiled or cooed to comfort you. Sometimes all the babies cried at once, and the nurses hurried to help each one of you.

You might have fussed when you were tired, but soon you got used to the noise and activity of the children around you. You probably learned to sleep through anything!

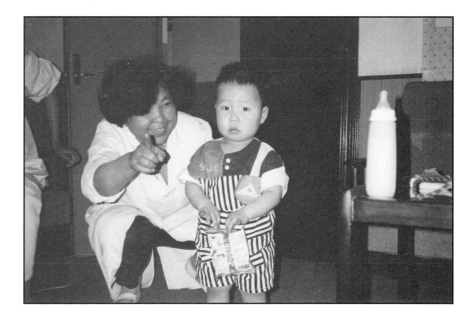

Much of the time you took naps, or explored the world around you. First you explored with your eyes and ears, watching the nurses walk past your crib and listening to their voices. There may have been a nurse you especially liked and who especially liked you—a nurse who made you smile and laugh.

After a while you started exploring with your arms and legs, sucking on your fingers, touching the blankets and the child next to you, and kicking with your legs. (But remember, if it was winter you were probably wrapped in so many clothes it was hard to move!)

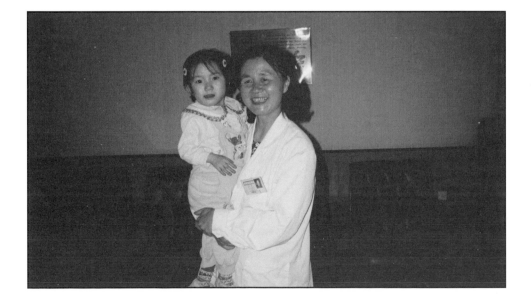

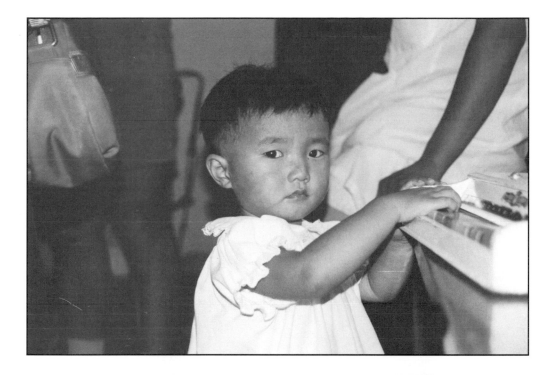

If you stayed in the orphanage until you were a little older, you probably learned to pull yourself up in your crib, eat rice and soup with a spoon, and say some Chinese words. You played and learned with the other children, and may have helped the nurses take care of the babies.

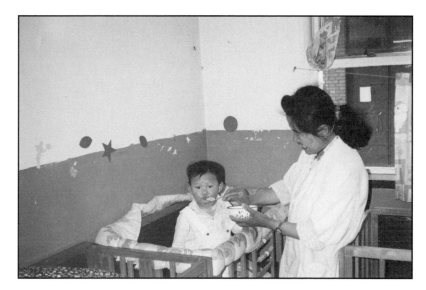

It's possible that the orphanage asked a nearby family to take care of you while you waited for your new family. This family, called a foster family, may have lived on a farm or possibly in a city. Like many Chinese families, your foster family may have included a child, a mother and father, and grandparents. Everybody helped to care for you until your new family could come to China. The orphanage gave your foster family money to buy clothing and food for you.

Your foster grandparents watched you at home, or your foster mother put you in a bamboo baby stroller and took you along as she did her daily chores. You ate the same kinds of things as the children in the orphanage, and yes, you probably wore split pants.

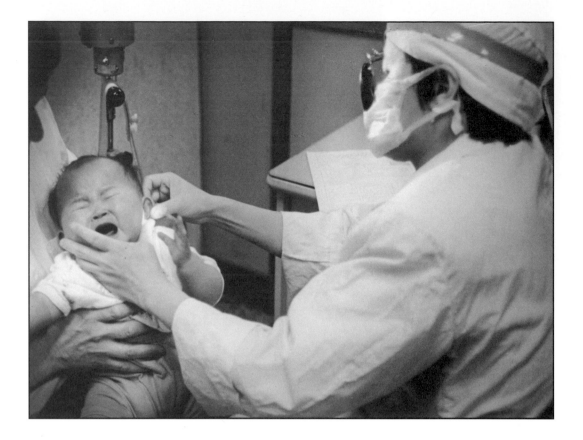

One day during this part of your story two important things happened. First, you were checked by a doctor. The doctor filled out a form about your health, including your height and weight. Then, you had your picture taken.

You might have squirmed when the doctor checked you, or blinked in surprise at the bright camera flash. You didn't realize it at the time, but the doctor's report and the photo would become important pieces of your story. You may even have seen them. They allowed your new family to find out about you.

You see, everyone who helped care for you—your birthparents, the person who brought you to the orphanage, the orphanage nurses, the foster family, the doctor—wanted one thing for you. More than anything else, they wanted you to have a family that would be yours forever. All these people knew that somewhere there was a family for you, maybe in China, or maybe even in another country in the world.

So, your orphanage sent your photo and health report to the Chinese officials in charge of adoptions. These officials also got information from families who needed children, and then worked hard to match just the right child and family.

Far across the ocean, your family was writing a letter, and filling out lots of papers. They told the officials in China how much they wanted to adopt a child just like you.

Then one day, after a long time of eager waiting, your family received a precious package. In this package there was a doctor's report, and a photograph of a beautiful child. That child was you! Oh, how your parents cried with joy, and how much they wanted to hold you right away!

With great excitement they prepared for that wonderful day when they would arrive in China to meet you.

32

When the people who took care of you in China heard that your family was coming, they were so glad for you. On the appointed day, your nurses dressed you as best they could to meet your family. They wondered who your family might be and what they might look like. If there were other children at the orphanage also meeting their new families, the nurses hurried to prepare all of you for the big day.

Your nurses, or someone from your foster family, then carried you to meet your new family. Your mom or dad, or both, may have actually come to the orphanage to meet you. Or they might have waited for you at their hotel, or at a government office. If the orphanage was far away from where your family was staying, your nurses bundled you into a car, or maybe a bus or train, for the long ride to the city where your new family was waiting.

It was quite a moment when you were first placed in your mom's or dad's arms. They had waited and hoped so long to hold you for the first time, and now here you were! They couldn't wait to get to know you. Of course you may have been scared or confused at first by these strange new faces.

The people who had cared for you were sad because they had to say good-bye, but they were so happy that now you had a family to care for you and love you for the rest of your life. They knew that you were in good hands. They were right!

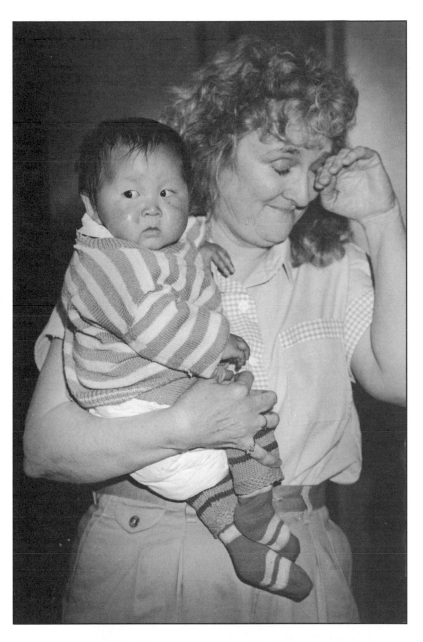

You have probably heard
the rest of your story.

Your family signed
papers saying they
wanted to adopt you.
They received your
birth certificate and
applied for your
passport.

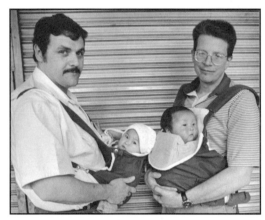

Your family also spent some time exploring China, the special country of your birth.

With each moment they
got to know you better.

Finally your family got permission to leave China with you.
Imagine their excitement as you all boarded the airplane
that would take you to your new home!

Many friends and family members waited eagerly for your arrival. You were starting a new and exciting chapter in your story, and they were so glad to be part of it.

To all the people in China who were part of your story before you joined your family—your birth parents, the nurses and other workers in the orphanage, perhaps a foster family—you were an important and special person. They cared for you and made decisions for you as best they could. You are still in their hearts. May you keep them in your heart as you grow.

Your story began in China, and it is very special.

About the author and photographer:

Sara Dorow has spent twenty years in Asia, three of those teaching and studying in China. After managing an East Asian adoption program for several years, she (and others) decided she didn't know enough. Sara is currently studying for her Ph.D. in Sociology, but is always looking for an excuse to cross the Pacific.

Stephen Wunrow is a freelance photographer who lives in St. Paul, Minnesota, but increasingly thinks maybe he should live in Asia. His wife and three children, two of whom were adopted from Korea, suffer him gladly and don't think he's totally crazy, most of the time. His photos also illustrate *When You Were Born in Korea*.

For further information and support, here are two resources of particular value to readers of this book:

Adoptive Families of America (AFA) is the largest non-profit membership organization in the United States serving adoptive and prospective adoptive families. Over 20,000 dedicated parents and adoption professionals have already joined. Whether you have adopted children or wish to adopt, AFA can provide you with a wealth of information, services, and support. From helping you find the right adoption agency to putting you in touch with other adoptive parents who are eager to share their experiences with you, AFA can help! You can contact AFA at 1-800-372-3300, or write to 3333 Highway 100 North, Minneapolis, MN 55422.

As a member of Adoptive Families of America, you will receive helpful information, invaluable resources, and support. Adoptive Families Magazine is a lively, upbeat bimonthly magazine that keeps you informed about current adoption news and parenting issues. Each 88-page, full-color issue brings articles written by adoptive parents and adoption professionals with timely information, practical parenting tips, and more. AFA also offers a listing of local support groups, including all current local chapters of Families with Children from China; a member helpline (call (612) 535-4829 for this service); and a free parenting resource catalog, with over 450 of the best adoption and ethnic heritage books, tapes, and dolls along with resources on parenting and self-esteem. In addition, AFA sponsors national adoption conferences, with workshops by expert adoptive parents and adoption professionals. Advocacy AFA represents your concerns and the concerns of children without permanent families by serving on national committees, proposing legislation, and consulting with Congress and federal agencies. AFA also has Aid to Children: a portion of your membership dollars goes to those in greatest need, the children. Each year, grants in aid are made to programs serving children in need of permanent homes all over the globe.

Families with Children from China (FCC) is an organization of families who have adopted children from China. It is a network of parent support groups in the United States, Canada, and the United Kingdom with the goal of providing support for families who have adopted in China, and to provide information to prospective parents.

Virtually all FCC chapters share the following three goals: To support families who've adopted in China through post-adoption and Chinese culture programs; To encourage adoption from China and support waiting families; To advocate for and support children remaining in orphanages in China. FCC chapters generally organize some or all of the following activities: newsletters, membership directories, family picnics and pot-luck suppers, celebrations of Chinese festivals and holidays, pre-adoption information meetings, playgroups, Chinese language and culture classes for children, parent speakers.

Families with Children from China does not have a national headquarters, but is an association of local chapters, so you should inquire locally to find the chapter nearest you. For those with computer access to the Internet, FCC maintains an excellent and very helpful site on the World Wide Web (http://fwcc.org), which can provide a great deal of useful information, as well as contacts for local chapters. FCC's New York chapter offers an "Adopting in China" packet, providing an overview of the law, costs, process, and requirements to adopt, and including a list of recent adopters (organized by city in China, agency or route, date, special issues of adoption) who are willing to talk by phone to prospective adopters about their experience. It's available from FCC-New York by sending a stamped self-addressed envelope to FCC, c/o Joe Kelly, 248 W. 105th Street, NY, NY 10025, or call 1-212-579-0115.

Photo Index and Annotations. All photos by Stephen Wunrow except as noted below.

Front cover: (top) the Great Wall at Mutianyu, (bottom) child in Hangzhou, Chinese characters translate as "When you were born in China". Title Pg. (top) school children in Hangzhou, (bottom) pavilion in Jingshan Park. Pg. 1 (top) child meeting her adoptive mother, (center left) orphanage nurse with child, (center right) boy near West Lake, Hangzhou, (bottom) school children before the start of classes, Hangzhou. Pg. 2 (top) Forbidden City, Beijing, (center left) Buddha sculpture at Lingyin Si (Temple of Inspired Seclusion) near Hangzhou, (center right) young boy at streetside cafe, Hangzhou, (bottom) lake in Zhejiang province. Pg. 3 outside the notary office, Hangzhou, (bottom) Tiananmen (Gate of Heavenly Peace), Beijing. Pg. 4 (top) back streets, Hangzhou, (bottom) boy reaching for tangerines, Hangzhou. Pg. 5 fishing on the canal in Hangzhou, (center) school children dancing before class, Hangzhou, (bottom) bicycles parked by factories with slogan reading "Go happily to work and return safely home." Pg. 6 (top) Lama Temple, Beijing, (center) burning incense at Lingyin Temple, Hangzhou, (bottom) Temple of Heaven, Beijing. Pg. 7 the Great Wall at Mutianyu. Pg. 8 (top) old neighborhood in Beijing, (center) mother and child in northeast China, photo by Sara Dorow, (bottom) apartment buildings in Hangzhou. Pg. 9 (top) bicycle parking lot with sign encouraging a clean environment, (bottom left) cafe, Hangzhou, (bottom right) school children, Beijing. Pg. 10 (top) apartment construction, Beijing, (bottom) cyclist, Guangzhou. Pg. 11 (top center) Coke ad, Hangzhou, (top right) one of many McDonald's Restaurants in Beijing, (center) tourists from Shanghai visiting Hangzhou, (bottom) rural scene, photo by Stephen Syrjala. Pg. 12 (top) the morning commute, Hangzhou, (bottom) apartments in Guangzhou. Pg. 13 (top) mother and child by a billboard encouraging family planning, (center and bottom) families in Hangzhou. Pg. 14 (top) fishing for carp at Ditan Park, Beijing, (center) mom and daughter, Hangzhou, (bottom) three generation family near the Great Wall at Mutianyu. Pg. 15 (top) school children, Hangzhou, (center left) father and son at Yellow Dragon Caves, Hangzhou, (center right) son and mother near the Great Wall at Mutianyu. Pg.16 (top) school children, Beijing, (bottom) school child, Hangzhou. Pg. 17 Special needs children, top photo by Sara Dorow, (bottom left) nurse and child in Suzhou orphanage, photo by Deborah Talen. Pg. 18 (top) mother and child, Beijing, (bottom) a theater in Zhejiang province. Pg. 19 (top) train station, Hangzhou, (bottom) a police station in Hangzhou. Pg. 20 at an orphanage in Suzhou, photos by Deborah Talen. Pg. 21 orphanage and nurses, central China, bottom photo by Deborah Talen. Pg. 22 children and nurses at orphanage in northern China. Pg. 23 Children in orphanage, central China, photo by Stephen Syrjala. Pg. 24 children with nurses, top photo by Deborah Talen. Pg. 25 children and nurses. Pg. 26 (top) orphanage, central China, photo by Stephen Syrjala, (bottom) child and nurse, northern China. Pg. 27 orphanage scenes, top photo by Deborah Talen. Pg. 28 family in Zhejiang province. Pg. 29 (top) bamboo stroller and occupant, Ditan Park, Beijing, (bottom) father holding child with split pants, Zhejiang province. Pg. 30 (top) visiting a clinic in Guangzhou. Pg. 31 (top) new mom meets her daughter and nurse, (bottom left) Chinese officials, (bottom right) the first cuddle with mom. Pg. 32 (top) bonding with dad, (bottom) typical referral photo and medical form. Pg. 33 (top) leaving an orphanage in central China, (bottom) walking in Hangzhou. Pg. 34 parents with children in Hangzhou. Pg. 35 meeting children for the first time, Hangzhou. Pg. 36 (top and center) doing adoption paperwork, (bottom) making a footprint. Pg. 37 (top) it's official! (bottom) group of new families. Pg. 38 (top) curious Chinese grandmas, Hangzhou, (center) dads getting the hang of things, Hangzhou, (bottom) early morning tai chi near West Lake, Hangzhou. Pg. 39 (top) Lingyin Temple near Hangzhou, (center) in a pedicab, Hangzhou, (bottom) dinner time, Hangzhou. Pg. 40 (top) Guangzhou airport, (bottom left) on the way home, (bottom right) waiting for new baby sister to arrive, St. Paul, Minnesota. Pg. 41 (top) waiting for new little sister to arrive, St. Paul, MN, (bottom) mom and daughter welcome new baby sister, St. Paul, MN. Pg. 42 The adoption class of May, 1996. Back cover: Temple of Heaven, Beijing.